Dublin Travel Guide 2023

2023

Perfect Dublin Vacation Planning: Tips & Recommendations 2023

Robbin Charles

DISCLAIMER

While we have made every effort to ensure that the information provided in this travel guide is accurate and up-to-date, we cannot guarantee that all details are current, complete, or error-free. The recommendations and tips provided are intended as a guide only and may not be suitable for everyone. It is always important to research and verify information independently, particularly regarding transportation schedules, admission prices, and hours of operation for attractions and businesses. The publisher and author are not responsible for any losses, injuries, or damages that may occur as a result of using this guide. Travelers are advised to exercise caution and make informed decisions when planning and embarking on their trips.

TABLE OF CONTENTS

Introduction

- Welcome to Dublin
- About this Guide
- Getting Around Dublin

Exploring Dublin

- Must-See Attractions
- Hidden Gems
- Dublin's Neighborhoods

Food and Drink

- Irish Cuisine
- Traditional Pubs
- Modern Bars and Restaurants

Entertainment and Nightlife

- Music Venues

- Theater and Performing Arts
- Nightclubs and Late-Night Bars

Outdoor Activities
- Parks and Gardens
- Hiking and Biking Trails
- Water Activities

Shopping and Souvenirs
- Dublin's Shopping Districts
- Unique Souvenirs

Accommodation
- Where to Stay in Dublin
- Hotels, Hostels, and Vacation Rentals

Day Trips from Dublin
- Coastal Towns

- Historical Sites
- Scenic Drives

Practical Information

- Transportation
- Money and Tipping
- Safety and Security

Conclusion

- Final Thoughts and Recommendations
- Dublin Travel Checklist

INTRODUCTION

Welcome to Dublin

Welcome to Dublin, the capital city of Ireland! Dublin is a vibrant and cosmopolitan city, with a rich history, a lively cultural scene, and a friendly and welcoming atmosphere. Situated on the east coast of Ireland, Dublin is home to over 1.2 million people and attracts millions of visitors each year.

Dublin has a long and fascinating history, with evidence of human settlement dating back over 7,000 years. The city has been the site of many important events throughout history, including the Battle of

Clontarf in 1014, the establishment of Trinity College in 1592, and the Easter Rising of 1916, which led to Ireland's independence from Britain.

Today, Dublin is a modern and bustling city, with a thriving economy, a vibrant nightlife, and a wide range of cultural attractions. Visitors can explore the city's many museums and galleries, including the National Museum.

About this Guide

This guide is designed to help you discover and explore the many sights and experiences that Dublin has to offer. Whether you are a first-time visitor or a seasoned traveler, this guide will provide you with valuable information and tips to make the most of your time in the city.

In this guide, you will find detailed information on Dublin's top attractions, including historic landmarks, cultural institutions, and natural wonders. You will also find recommendations for the best restaurants, pubs, and shops in the city, as well as insider tips on how to navigate Dublin's streets and neighborhoods.

Additionally, this guide will provide you with practical information on transportation, accommodation, and safety, so you can feel confident and comfortable as you explore Dublin. We want to make sure that you have a memorable and enjoyable experience in this wonderful city, and we hope that this guide will be a helpful resource for you.

Getting Around Dublin

Getting around Dublin is easy, with a variety of transportation options available to visitors. The city is well-connected by buses, trams, trains, and taxis, and there are also options for cycling and walking.

Dublin's public transportation system is operated by the national transport authority, and includes buses, trams, and trains. The most popular form of public transport in Dublin is the bus, with a comprehensive network of routes covering the city and surrounding areas. The tram system, known as the Luas, also provides convenient and efficient transportation between different parts of the city, while the suburban rail network offers fast and convenient connections to towns and villages outside of Dublin.

Taxis are also widely available in Dublin, and can be hailed on the street or booked in advance. Additionally, there are numerous bike rental options available throughout the city, making cycling a convenient and enjoyable way to explore Dublin's streets and neighborhoods.

For those who prefer to walk, Dublin is a compact and pedestrian-friendly city, with many of the city's top attractions located within walking distance of each other. Walking tours are also a popular way to explore Dublin, with guided tours available for a range of interests and themes.

Overall, getting around Dublin is convenient and easy, with a range of transportation options available to suit every preference and budget.

Exploring Dublin

Must-See Attractions

Dublin is a city rich in history, culture, and natural beauty, with many must-see attractions that visitors should not miss. Here are some of the top attractions to explore in Dublin:

- Guinness Storehouse - This iconic brewery is one of Dublin's most popular attractions, with a seven-story museum and interactive exhibits showcasing the history of Guinness beer. Visitors can also enjoy panoramic views of the city from the Gravity Bar on the top floor.

- Trinity College - Founded in 1592, Trinity College is one of Ireland's oldest and most prestigious universities, and home to the famous Book of Kells, an illuminated manuscript dating back to the 9th century.

- Dublin Castle - This historic castle has played a pivotal role in Irish history for over 800 years, serving as the seat of British rule in Ireland until independence in 1922. Visitors can explore the castle's opulent state apartments and learn about its fascinating history.

- St. Patrick's Cathedral - Founded in 1191, this stunning cathedral is one of Dublin's most iconic landmarks, and the largest church in Ireland. Visitors can admire its Gothic architecture, beautiful stained-glass windows, and learn about its connection to Ireland's patron saint, St. Patrick.

- Phoenix Park - One of the largest enclosed city parks in Europe, Phoenix Park is a tranquil oasis in the heart of Dublin, with beautiful gardens, wildlife, and historic monuments. Visitors can also see the residence of the President of Ireland, Áras an

Uachtaráin, located within the park.

- National Museum of Ireland – This museum offers a fascinating glimpse into Ireland's history and culture, with exhibitions on archaeology, decorative arts, and natural history. Highlights include the Ardagh Chalice, a masterpiece of early Irish metalwork, and the famous Tara Brooch, a symbol of Ireland's ancient Celtic heritage.

These are just a few of the many must-see attractions in Dublin. Whether you're interested in history, culture, or natural beauty, Dublin has something to offer for every visitor.

Hidden Gems

In addition to its well-known attractions, Dublin is also home to many hidden gems that are off the beaten path but are equally fascinating and worth exploring. Here are some of the top hidden gems in Dublin:

- Marsh's Library - This hidden gem is one of Dublin's oldest public libraries, founded in 1701. The library houses an impressive collection of rare and historic books, including works by Shakespeare, Newton, and Swift.

- The Little Museum of Dublin - Located in a Georgian townhouse on St. Stephen's Green, this charming museum tells the story of Dublin's history through a collection of personal artifacts and memorabilia donated by the city's residents.

- The Iveagh Gardens - This tranquil park is a hidden oasis in the heart of Dublin, with beautiful landscaped gardens, fountains, and sculptures. The park is home to several events throughout the year, including concerts, theater performances, and art exhibitions.

- Kilmainham Gaol - This former prison is a haunting reminder of

Ireland's turbulent past, serving as a site of imprisonment and execution during the country's struggle for independence. Guided tours offer a fascinating glimpse into the prison's history and the lives of its inmates.

- The Dublin Ghost Bus Tour - This unique tour takes visitors on a journey through Dublin's spooky side, visiting haunted sites and sharing tales of the city's ghosts and ghouls.

- The National Leprechaun Museum - This whimsical museum explores the folklore and mythology of Ireland, with exhibits and interactive displays on leprechauns, fairies, and other creatures of Irish legend.

These hidden gems offer a unique and fascinating perspective on Dublin's history, culture, and folklore, and are well worth a visit for those looking to explore the city's lesser-known attractions.

Dublin's Neighborhoods

Dublin is a vibrant and diverse city, with many distinct neighborhoods that each offer their own unique character and charm. Here are some of the top neighborhoods to explore in Dublin:

- Temple Bar – This lively neighborhood is known for its colorful streets, lively pubs, and vibrant arts scene. Visitors can explore the many galleries, theaters, and street performers that line the cobblestone streets, or sample traditional Irish cuisine and live music at one of the many pubs and restaurants.

- Grafton Street - This bustling shopping district is home to many of Dublin's top shops and boutiques, as well as street performers and musicians. Visitors can enjoy a leisurely stroll down the pedestrianized street and take in the lively atmosphere.

- Stoneybatter - This trendy neighborhood is a favorite among locals, with a thriving food and drink scene, unique shops, and colorful street art. Visitors can explore the many independent boutiques and cafes that line the streets, or sample craft beer and artisanal cuisine at

one of the many local pubs and
restaurants.

- Ballsbridge - This affluent
  neighborhood is home to many
  historic mansions and
  embassies, as well as the iconic
  Aviva Stadium. Visitors can
  explore the picturesque streets
  and gardens, or enjoy a scenic
  walk along the Grand Canal.

- Dublin Docklands - This
  revitalized neighborhood is a hub
  of innovation and technology,
  with many of the world's top tech
  companies headquartered here.
  Visitors can explore the sleek
  modern architecture, take in a

show at the Bord Gáis Energy
Theatre, or enjoy a leisurely walk
along the River Liffey.

These are just a few of the many
neighborhoods that make Dublin such
a vibrant and diverse city. Each
neighborhood offers its own unique
atmosphere and attractions, making
Dublin a city that is well worth
exploring.

Food and Drink

Irish Cuisine

Irish cuisine is known for its hearty, comforting dishes that are often made with simple, locally sourced ingredients. Here are some of the top Irish dishes to try when visiting Dublin:

- Irish Stew - This classic dish is made with lamb or beef, potatoes, onions, and carrots, slow-cooked in a rich broth until tender and flavorful.

- Boxty - These traditional Irish potato pancakes are made with grated potatoes, flour, and milk or buttermilk, and can be served sweet or savory.

- Coddle - This hearty stew is made with sausages, bacon, onions, and potatoes, slow-cooked in a flavorful broth until the ingredients are tender and the flavors are well blended.

- Dublin Bay Prawns - Also known as langoustines, these succulent shellfish are a specialty of the Dublin Bay area and are often served grilled or boiled with garlic butter.

- Irish Brown Bread - This hearty bread is made with wholemeal flour, buttermilk, and baking soda, giving it a dense, nutty flavor and a satisfying texture.

In addition to these traditional dishes, Dublin also offers a thriving food and drink scene, with many top restaurants, cafes, and bars serving up creative and innovative cuisine. Visitors can sample everything from modern Irish cuisine to international flavors, and can enjoy a pint of Guinness or a glass of Irish whiskey at one of the many cozy pubs that line the city's streets.

Traditional Pubs

Dublin is known for its traditional pubs, which offer a cozy and welcoming atmosphere where locals and visitors alike can enjoy a pint of Guinness and some traditional Irish pub fare. Here are some of the top traditional pubs to visit in Dublin:

- The Brazen Head - This historic pub dates back to 1198 and is one of the oldest pubs in Ireland. Visitors can enjoy live music, hearty pub fare, and a pint of Guinness or Irish whiskey in a cozy and historic setting.

- The Long Hall - This elegant Victorian-era pub is known for its ornate decor, including polished wood paneling, mirrored walls, and a stunning stained glass ceiling. Visitors can enjoy a pint of Guinness or a classic Irish whiskey in a sophisticated and atmospheric setting.

- The Cobblestone - This traditional pub is a favorite among locals, with live music sessions, traditional Irish music, and a warm and welcoming atmosphere. Visitors can enjoy a pint of Guinness or a local craft beer, and sample some traditional Irish pub fare.

- The Stag's Head - This historic pub is known for its ornate Victorian decor, including carved wood paneling, stained glass windows, and a stunning marble bar. Visitors can enjoy a pint of Guinness or Irish whiskey, and sample some traditional Irish dishes such as beef and Guinness stew.

- O'Donoghue's - This iconic pub is famous for its live music sessions, which have featured some of Ireland's most famous musicians over the years. Visitors can enjoy a pint of Guinness or a local craft beer, and soak up the lively and atmospheric atmosphere.

These traditional pubs offer a unique and authentic glimpse into Irish pub culture, and are well worth a visit for anyone looking to experience the warm and welcoming hospitality that Dublin is known for.

Modern Bars and Restaurants

Dublin's food and drink scene is not just limited to traditional pubs and Irish cuisine. The city also boasts a range of modern bars and restaurants, offering innovative and international cuisine and creative cocktails. Here are some of the top modern bars and restaurants to check out in Dublin:

- 777 - This trendy Mexican restaurant serves up delicious tacos, tostadas, and cocktails in a stylish and vibrant setting.

- The Exchequer - This modern gastro pub offers a menu of creative and innovative dishes, including sharing plates, burgers, and steaks, along with an extensive drinks menu featuring craft beer, wine, and cocktails.

- The Blind Pig - This speakeasy-style bar is hidden away behind a door marked only by a brass pig, and offers a range of creative cocktails and small plates in a cozy and atmospheric setting.

- Forest Avenue - This Michelin-starred restaurant serves up modern Irish cuisine with a focus on locally sourced

ingredients and creative flavor
combinations.

- The Vintage Cocktail Club - This
  stylish cocktail bar is located in a
  hidden location above a vintage
  clothing store, and offers a range
  of creative and inventive
  cocktails along with a small bites
  menu.

These modern bars and restaurants
offer a refreshing alternative to
traditional Irish cuisine and pub
culture, and are perfect for anyone
looking to experience the cutting-edge
of Dublin's food and drink scene.

Entertainment and Nightlife

Music Venues

Dublin is known for its vibrant nightlife and entertainment scene, and music venues are a big part of that. Here are some of the top music venues in Dublin:

- The Olympia Theatre: The Olympia Theatre is a historic venue that has been a mainstay of Dublin's entertainment scene since it opened in 1879. It has hosted many famous acts over the years, including Adele, David Bowie, and Radiohead.

- Whelan's: Whelan's is a popular venue for both up-and-coming and established artists. It has a cozy, intimate atmosphere and is known for its great sound quality.

- The Academy: The Academy is a multi-level venue that hosts a variety of events, including concerts, club nights, and comedy shows. It has a capacity of 1,500 and has hosted acts like The Script and Arctic Monkeys.

- Vicar Street: Vicar Street is a large, modern venue that hosts a wide range of events, including music, comedy, and theater. It has a capacity of 1,500 and has hosted acts like Bob Dylan, Sinead O'Connor, and Morrissey.

- Button Factory: The Button Factory is a versatile venue that can accommodate up to 750 people. It hosts a variety of events, including live music, DJ sets, and comedy shows.

- The Workman's Club: The Workman's Club is a trendy venue that hosts a variety of events, including live music, comedy, and club nights. It has a capacity of 450 and has hosted acts like Hozier and Villagers.

- The Grand Social: The Grand
  Social is a multi-purpose venue
  that hosts live music, club nights,
  and other events. It has a
  capacity of 400 and has hosted
  acts like The Coronas and
  Damien Dempsey.

Overall, Dublin has a fantastic music
scene, with a wide variety of venues
and acts to suit all tastes. Whether
you're into rock, pop, folk, or
electronic music, you're sure to find
something to enjoy in Dublin's vibrant
music scene.

Theater and Performing Arts

Dublin is known for its rich cultural heritage, and the city's theater and performing arts scene is no exception. Here are some of the top venues and companies for theater and performing arts in Dublin:

- The Abbey Theatre: The Abbey Theatre is Ireland's national theater and is located in the heart of Dublin. It was founded in 1904 and has a long history of producing groundbreaking Irish plays. It has two stages, the Abbey Stage and the Peacock Stage, and hosts a variety of productions throughout the year.

- The Gate Theatre: The Gate Theatre is one of Dublin's oldest theaters and has a reputation for producing high-quality drama. It was founded in 1928 and has hosted many famous actors over the years, including Orson Welles and Michael Gambon.

- The Gaiety Theatre: The Gaiety Theatre is a historic venue that has been a mainstay of Dublin's entertainment scene since it opened in 1871. It hosts a variety of productions, including musicals, dramas, and comedies.

- The Project Arts Centre: The Project Arts Centre is a contemporary arts center that hosts a variety of experimental theater, dance, and performance art. It also has a gallery space that showcases contemporary visual art.

- The Dublin Theatre Festival: The Dublin Theatre Festival is an annual event that takes place in September and October. It showcases the best of Irish and international theater and attracts theater enthusiasts from around the world.

- The Irish National Opera: The Irish National Opera is Ireland's national opera company and performs a variety of operas throughout the year. It was founded in 2018 and has quickly become a staple of Dublin's cultural scene.

- The Dublin Fringe Festival: The Dublin Fringe Festival is an annual festival that takes place in September and showcases the best of Dublin's avant-garde theater and performance art. It features a variety of events, including theater, dance, music, and comedy.

Overall, Dublin has a thriving theater and performing arts scene that offers something for everyone. Whether you're interested in classic drama or cutting-edge experimental theater, you're sure to find something to enjoy in Dublin's vibrant performing arts community.

Nightclubs and Late-Night Bars

Dublin is a vibrant city with a thriving entertainment and nightlife scene. There are plenty of options for those looking for nightclubs and late-night bars to enjoy.

Nightclubs in Dublin offer a variety of music genres to cater to different tastes. Some of the most popular clubs include The Wright Venue, Opium Club, and District 8. The Wright Venue is a multi-room club with state-of-the-art sound and lighting systems, while Opium Club has a rooftop terrace and hosts international DJs. District 8 is located in a former warehouse and is known for its techno and electronic music.

Late-night bars in Dublin are also a popular option for those looking for a more laid-back atmosphere. The Temple Bar area is particularly well-known for its traditional Irish pubs, such as The Temple Bar, which is a tourist attraction in its own right, and O'Donoghue's, which has a long history of hosting live music performances.

If you're looking for a more modern and trendy bar scene, areas like Camden Street and South William Street offer a variety of options. The Bernard Shaw, which has an outdoor garden and hosts regular events, and The Vintage Cocktail Club, a speakeasy-style bar with a hidden entrance, are both popular choices.

It's important to note that Dublin has strict licensing laws, so it's always a good idea to plan ahead and check opening hours before heading out. Additionally, it's worth keeping in mind that some venues have dress codes and door policies, so it's always best to check in advance to avoid disappointment.

Overall, Dublin has a vibrant entertainment and nightlife scene with plenty of options for those looking for nightclubs and late-night bars.

Whether you're looking for traditional Irish pubs, trendy bars, or international DJs, you're sure to find something to suit your tastes in this exciting city.

Outdoor Activities

Parks and Gardens

Dublin, the capital city of Ireland, is known for its vibrant culture, rich history, and scenic landscapes. One of the best ways to experience the natural beauty of Dublin is by exploring its numerous parks and gardens. Here are some of the top outdoor activities to do in Dublin's parks and gardens:

1. Phoenix Park: Spanning over 1,700 acres, Phoenix Park is one of the largest urban parks in Europe. The park is home to several attractions, including Dublin Zoo, Áras an Uachtaráin (the official residence of

the President of Ireland), and the Wellington Monument. Visitors can also enjoy walking and cycling on the park's many trails, picnicking on the lawns, and even playing a round of golf at the park's golf course.

2. St. Stephen's Green: Located in the heart of Dublin's city center, St. Stephen's Green is a peaceful oasis amidst the bustling city streets. The park features beautifully manicured gardens, a lake with swans, and several sculptures and monuments. Visitors can relax on the lawns, feed the ducks, or take a stroll through the park's tree-lined paths.

3. National Botanic Gardens: The National Botanic Gardens is a must-visit for nature lovers. The gardens boast over 20,000 different plant species from around the world, including rare and endangered species. Visitors can explore the many greenhouses, take a guided tour, or simply enjoy a leisurely stroll through the gardens.

4. Merrion Square: Located in Dublin's Georgian Quarter, Merrion Square is a picturesque park with colorful flower beds and a statue of Oscar Wilde. The park is a popular spot for locals and tourists alike, who come to enjoy the tranquil atmosphere and admire the

Georgian architecture that surrounds the square.

5. Iveagh Gardens: Tucked away in a quiet corner of Dublin's city center, Iveagh Gardens is a hidden gem that many visitors overlook. The gardens feature a maze, a waterfall, and a striking archway called the "Rustic Grotto." Visitors can also enjoy free outdoor concerts and events during the summer months.

These are just a few of the many parks and gardens to explore in Dublin. Whether you're looking for a peaceful retreat or an exciting adventure, Dublin's outdoor spaces offer something for everyone.

Hiking and Biking Trails

Dublin, the capital city of Ireland, is a great destination for outdoor enthusiasts, with many hiking and biking trails available for visitors to explore. Here are some of the top outdoor activities for hiking and biking in Dublin:

1. Wicklow Way: The Wicklow Way is a famous long-distance hiking trail that spans over 130 kilometers from Dublin to County Wicklow. The trail takes visitors through stunning landscapes, including forests, mountains, and lakes, and is a great way to experience the natural beauty of the region.

Visitors can hike the entire trail or choose to tackle shorter sections.

2. Howth Cliff Path Loop: The Howth Cliff Path Loop is a popular hiking trail that takes visitors on a scenic journey around the Howth peninsula, just outside of Dublin. The trail offers stunning views of the Irish Sea and the surrounding coastline, and visitors can stop off at the historic Howth Castle and Gardens or the fishing village of Howth for a bite to eat.

3. Phoenix Park Bike Trail: For visitors who prefer biking over hiking, the Phoenix Park Bike Trail is a great option. The trail takes visitors on a 5-kilometer loop around Phoenix Park,

one of the largest urban parks in Europe. The trail offers beautiful views of the park's gardens, lakes, and historic buildings, and is suitable for cyclists of all levels.

4. Dodder Greenway: The Dodder Greenway is a new 14-kilometer walking and cycling trail that follows the River Dodder through south Dublin. The trail offers a peaceful escape from the city and takes visitors through several parks, including Bushy Park and Ringsend Park. Visitors can also stop off at local cafes and restaurants along the way.

5. Dublin Mountains Way: The Dublin Mountains Way is a 43-kilometer

hiking and biking trail that takes visitors through the mountains and forests just outside of Dublin. The trail offers stunning views of the city and the surrounding countryside, and visitors can stop off at the picturesque villages of Tallaght and Bohernabreena along the way.

These are just a few of the many hiking and biking trails to explore in Dublin. Whether you're looking for a challenging adventure or a leisurely ride, Dublin's outdoor spaces offer something for everyone.

Water Activities

Dublin, the capital city of Ireland, is situated on the east coast of the country, providing visitors with plenty of opportunities to enjoy water-based activities. Here are some of the top outdoor activities for water lovers in Dublin:

1. Kayaking and Canoeing: Dublin offers several opportunities for kayaking and canoeing, with many scenic routes available along the city's rivers and canals. Visitors can explore the city from a different perspective, taking in sights such as Dublin Castle and St. Patrick's Cathedral from the water.

2. Sailing: Dublin Bay is a great location for sailing, with several sailing schools offering lessons and rental options for visitors. Experienced sailors can also take part in racing events that take place throughout the year.

3. Stand-up Paddleboarding (SUP): Stand-up paddleboarding has become increasingly popular in Dublin in recent years, with several companies offering lessons and rental options. The calm waters of the Grand Canal or the River Liffey are perfect for beginners, while more experienced paddlers can explore Dublin Bay.

4. Wild Swimming: For the more adventurous, wild swimming is a unique experience that allows visitors to take a dip in the Irish Sea or one of the many natural swimming spots in the Dublin Mountains. While it's important to take necessary precautions and only swim in safe locations, wild swimming offers a refreshing way to experience the natural beauty of Dublin.

5. Fishing: Dublin offers several options for fishing enthusiasts, with opportunities for sea fishing along the coast or freshwater fishing in the city's canals and rivers. Visitors can also take part in fishing charters or guided tours

to learn more about the best fishing spots and techniques.

These are just a few of the many water-based activities to enjoy in Dublin. Whether you're looking for a thrilling adventure or a peaceful escape, Dublin's waterways offer something for everyone.

Shopping and Souvenirs

Dublin's Shopping Districts

Dublin is a fantastic destination for anyone looking to indulge in some retail therapy or pick up a few souvenirs to take back home. The city boasts a diverse range of shopping districts, each with its unique character and charm. Here are some of the best shopping districts in Dublin:

1. Grafton Street:
Grafton Street is one of Dublin's most popular shopping districts, located in the heart of the city center. It's home to many high-end brands like Brown Thomas, Swarovski, and Ted Baker, as

well as popular Irish retailers like Avoca and Carraig Donn. The area is also home to street performers, musicians, and artists, making it a lively spot to spend a few hours browsing shops and people-watching.

2. Henry Street:
Henry Street is another bustling shopping district in Dublin's city center. It's home to several department stores like Arnotts and Dunnes Stores, as well as popular fashion retailers like H&M, Forever 21, and River Island. There are also several souvenir shops and smaller boutiques selling unique gifts and Irish crafts.

3. Temple Bar:

Temple Bar is Dublin's cultural quarter, famous for its vibrant nightlife, live music, and cultural events. However, it's also a great spot to pick up some souvenirs. There are several shops selling Irish-themed gifts, like Aran sweaters, Celtic jewelry, and handmade pottery. You'll also find several vintage shops and second-hand bookstores, making it a great spot for quirky finds.

4. Dublin Flea Market:
If you're looking for something truly unique, head to the Dublin Flea Market. It's held on the last Sunday of every month and features over 60 stalls selling everything from vintage clothing and furniture to handmade

crafts and artisanal food products. It's a great spot to pick up some one-of-a-kind souvenirs or gifts.

Overall, Dublin is a fantastic destination for anyone looking to shop or pick up some souvenirs. Whether you're after high-end fashion, Irish crafts, or quirky finds, there's something for everyone in Dublin's shopping districts.

Unique Souvenirs

Dublin, the capital city of Ireland, is a vibrant and bustling destination with plenty to see and do. For those looking to do some shopping and pick up some unique souvenirs to take home, Dublin offers a range of options.

One of the most popular areas for shopping in Dublin is Grafton Street. This pedestrianized shopping street is home to a wide range of shops, from high-end boutiques to more affordable high-street brands. You'll find everything from clothing and jewelry to books and souvenirs, and there's always a lively atmosphere.

When it comes to souvenirs, Dublin has plenty of unique options to choose from. Here are a few ideas:

1. Aran Sweaters: These thick, warm sweaters are made from wool and are a traditional Irish garment. You'll find them in many shops around Dublin, and they make for a cozy and practical souvenir.

2. Irish Whiskey: Ireland is famous for its whiskey, and there are many distilleries and shops around Dublin where you can pick up a bottle. Look out for brands like Jameson and Bushmills, or try something new and lesser-known.

3. Claddagh Rings: This traditional Irish ring features two hands holding a heart, with a crown on top. It symbolizes love, loyalty, and friendship, and is a popular gift for loved ones.

4. Irish Pottery: From handmade mugs to decorative plates, Irish pottery is a beautiful and functional souvenir. Look out for brands like Belleek and Nicholas Mosse, or visit the Dublin Pottery School to see local artists at work.

5. Guinness Merchandise: No trip to Dublin would be complete without trying a pint of Guinness, and there are plenty of opportunities to pick up some

Guinness-themed souvenirs. From t-shirts and hats to pint glasses and bottle openers, there's something for everyone.

Whether you're looking for a practical souvenir or a decorative item to remind you of your trip, Dublin has plenty of unique options to choose from. Just be sure to leave some space in your suitcase!

Accommodation

Where to Stay in Dublin

Dublin, the capital city of Ireland, is a popular tourist destination known for its lively atmosphere, rich culture, and historical landmarks. When it comes to finding a place to stay in Dublin, there are several options to consider, from budget-friendly hostels to luxurious hotels.

Here are some areas and accommodation options to consider when planning your stay in Dublin:

1. Temple Bar: Temple Bar is the most famous area of Dublin and is located in the city center. It is known for its vibrant nightlife, pubs, and restaurants. While staying in this area, you can easily walk to many of Dublin's top attractions, such as Trinity College, Dublin Castle, and the Guinness Storehouse. However, this area can be noisy at night, so if you're a light sleeper, you might want to consider staying elsewhere.

Accommodation options in Temple Bar: Temple Bar Inn, Barnacles Hostel, The Clarence Hotel

2. O'Connell Street: O'Connell Street is another central location in Dublin that

is close to many of the city's top attractions. It is a busy area with lots of shops, restaurants, and public transport links.

Accommodation options in O'Connell Street: The Gresham Hotel, The Pillar Hotel, Abigails Hostel

3. Dublin 2: Dublin 2 is a trendy area with many fashionable shops, cafes, and restaurants. It is close to St. Stephen's Green, a beautiful park in the heart of the city.

Accommodation options in Dublin 2: The Merrion Hotel, The Westbury Hotel, Generator Hostel

4. Dublin 4: Dublin 4 is a quieter area located to the south of the city center. It is a good choice if you want to be close to the city but prefer a more peaceful environment.

Accommodation options in Dublin 4: The InterContinental Dublin, The Clayton Hotel Ballsbridge, Pembroke Townhouse

5. Dublin Airport: If you're only in Dublin for a short period or have an early morning flight, staying near the airport is a good option. There are several hotels located close to Dublin Airport that offer free shuttle services to the terminal.

Accommodation options near Dublin Airport: The Radisson Blu Hotel Dublin Airport, The Clayton Hotel Dublin Airport, The Holiday Inn Express Dublin Airport.

When choosing where to stay in Dublin, it's important to consider your budget, the location, and your personal preferences. Dublin offers a range of accommodation options to suit different budgets and travel styles, so there's something for everyone.

Hotels, Hostels, and Vacation Rentals

Dublin is a vibrant city that welcomes a wide range of visitors every year, from budget backpackers to luxury seekers. When it comes to accommodation in Dublin, you'll find a variety of options to suit different budgets and preferences. Here are some popular options to consider:

1. Hotels: Dublin has a range of hotels to suit different budgets and travel styles, from budget-friendly options to luxury hotels. Many of the high-end hotels are located in the city center, close to top attractions and popular shopping districts. Some of the well-known luxury

hotels in Dublin include The Merrion, The Shelbourne, and The Westbury. If you're looking for a budget-friendly option, there are several chain hotels and budget hotels, such as Travelodge and Premier Inn.

2. Hostels: Hostels are a popular option for budget-conscious travelers and solo travelers. Dublin has several hostels scattered throughout the city, with some of the most popular located in the city center. Hostels are an excellent way to meet other travelers, and many offer communal areas, such as lounges, kitchens, and bars. Some of the top hostels in Dublin include Barnacles Hostel, Jacobs Inn, and Generator Hostel.

3. Vacation Rentals: Vacation rentals are becoming an increasingly popular option for travelers who want more space and privacy. Dublin has several vacation rentals, including apartments and houses, available to rent. Many vacation rentals are located in residential areas, away from the city center, and can be an excellent option for families or larger groups. Some popular vacation rental platforms include Airbnb and HomeAway.

4. Guesthouses and B&Bs: If you're looking for a more personalized and homely experience, guesthouses and B&Bs are a great option. These are often family-run businesses and offer a more intimate experience compared to larger hotels. Guesthouses and B&Bs are

typically located in residential areas or suburbs, and many offer a traditional Irish breakfast as part of the package. Some popular options include The Pembroke Townhouse, The Avondale House, and The Waterloo Lodge.

When choosing your accommodation in Dublin, it's important to consider your budget, preferred location, and travel style. Dublin offers a range of options, from high-end luxury hotels to budget-friendly hostels and vacation rentals, so you'll be able to find something that suits your needs.

Day Trips from Dublin

Coastal Towns

Dublin is a beautiful and vibrant city that has plenty to offer, but sometimes you may want to escape the hustle and bustle of city life and explore the beautiful coastal towns that surround it. These towns offer stunning views of the Irish Sea, charming seaside villages, historical landmarks, and plenty of outdoor activities. Here are some of the top day trips from Dublin to coastal towns:

1. Howth: Howth is a picturesque fishing village located just 30 minutes from Dublin's city center. It's a popular

spot for fishing, sailing, and hiking, with its stunning cliffs offering fantastic views of the surrounding area. You can also explore the historic Howth Castle and take a stroll through the colorful streets of the village, stopping to sample some of the delicious seafood in the local restaurants.

2. Dun Laoghaire: Dun Laoghaire is a seaside town that's just a short train ride away from Dublin. It's a popular destination for those who love watersports, with opportunities for kayaking, windsurfing, and sailing. The town is also home to the iconic East Pier, which offers stunning views

of Dublin Bay, and the historic
19th-century Dun Laoghaire Baths.

3. Bray: Bray is a charming seaside
town that's located just south of
Dublin. It's a popular spot for families,
with its amusement park, aquarium,
and beautiful beaches. The town also
boasts some excellent restaurants,
cafes, and pubs, making it a great place
to spend a relaxing day by the sea.

4. Malahide: Malahide is a picturesque
town that's located just north of
Dublin. It's home to the stunning
Malahide Castle, which dates back to
the 12th century, and boasts beautiful
gardens and a museum. The town is
also a popular spot for sailing and

fishing, and you can take a leisurely stroll along the marina or sample some of the delicious seafood in the local restaurants.

5. Skerries: Skerries is a charming coastal town that's located just north of Dublin. It's a popular destination for those who love watersports, with opportunities for sailing, kayaking, and windsurfing. The town also boasts some beautiful beaches, and you can take a stroll along the South Strand or explore the historic Skerries Mills.

Overall, there are plenty of beautiful coastal towns to explore on a day trip from Dublin. Whether you're interested in outdoor activities, history, or simply soaking up the seaside atmosphere, you're sure to find something to suit your interests.

Historical Sites

Dublin, the capital city of Ireland, is home to some of the country's most significant historical sites, ranging from ancient ruins to medieval castles and landmarks associated with the country's fight for independence. While there's plenty to explore in the city itself, there are also many worthwhile day trips to historical sites within easy reach of Dublin. Here are some top picks for historical day trips from Dublin:

1. Newgrange: Located in County Meath, about an hour's drive from Dublin, Newgrange is a prehistoric monument that's older than

Stonehenge and the Great Pyramids of Giza. It was built around 3200 BC and is an impressive example of Neolithic engineering. Visitors can take a guided tour of the site to learn more about its history and significance.

2. Glendalough: This beautiful valley in County Wicklow is home to an important monastic site that dates back to the 6th century. The ruins of a round tower, several churches, and a cemetery are still visible today. The surrounding landscape is also stunning, with hiking trails and lakes to explore.

3. Kilkenny Castle: Located in the charming medieval city of Kilkenny,

about two hours' drive from Dublin, Kilkenny Castle is a 12th-century fortress that was once home to the powerful Butler family. Visitors can take a guided tour of the castle's interior and explore the surrounding gardens and parkland.

4. Hill of Tara: Situated in County Meath, the Hill of Tara was once the seat of the High Kings of Ireland and is said to be the place where St. Patrick converted the pagan Irish to Christianity. Visitors can explore the site's ancient monuments, including the Mound of the Hostages and the Stone of Destiny.

5. Kilmainham Gaol: This former prison in Dublin was where many of Ireland's most famous political prisoners were held, including leaders of the 1916 Easter Rising. Today, it's a museum that offers guided tours of the cells and provides insight into Ireland's struggle for independence.

These are just a few of the historical day trips that are available from Dublin. Whether you're interested in ancient history, medieval castles, or modern politics, there's something for everyone within easy reach of the city.

Scenic Drives

Dublin, the capital city of Ireland, is surrounded by beautiful countryside and stunning coastal landscapes, making it an ideal location for scenic drives and day trips. Here are some suggestions for scenic drives that you can take from Dublin:

1. The Wicklow Mountains: Just a short drive from Dublin, the Wicklow Mountains are a popular destination for hikers and outdoor enthusiasts. The winding roads through the mountains offer stunning views of the rolling hills, tranquil lakes, and verdant forests. One of the most popular routes is the Wicklow Gap,

which takes you through the heart of the mountains and offers breathtaking vistas of the surrounding countryside.

2. The Wild Atlantic Way: The Wild Atlantic Way is a 2,500 km coastal driving route that stretches from Donegal in the north to Cork in the south. The route takes in some of the most spectacular coastal scenery in the world, with rugged cliffs, golden beaches, and charming fishing villages along the way. The section of the route that runs from Dublin to Galway is particularly beautiful, with stunning views of the Atlantic Ocean and the Connemara Mountains.

3. The Boyne Valley: The Boyne Valley is a historic region just north of Dublin that is home to some of Ireland's most ancient monuments. A scenic drive through the valley takes you past landmarks such as the Hill of Tara, Newgrange, and the Battle of the Boyne site. The rolling countryside, dotted with farms and quaint villages, is a peaceful and idyllic setting for a leisurely drive.

4. The Causeway Coastal Route: The Causeway Coastal Route is a 190 km drive along the stunning coastline of Northern Ireland, just a few hours' drive from Dublin. The route takes in iconic landmarks such as the Giant's Causeway, Carrick-a-Rede Rope

Bridge, and Dunluce Castle, as well as offering spectacular views of the rugged coastline and the wild Atlantic Ocean.

5. The Ring of Kerry: The Ring of Kerry is a 179 km circular route that takes in some of the most stunning scenery in Ireland. The route starts and ends in Killarney and takes in the rugged coastline, charming villages, and rolling hills of County Kerry. Highlights of the drive include the Skellig Islands, the Muckross House and Gardens, and the Gap of Dunloe.

Whether you're a nature lover, history buff, or just looking to get away from the city for a day, there are plenty of scenic drives and day trips to enjoy from Dublin.

Practical Information

Transportation

Dublin, the capital city of Ireland, has a variety of transportation options to help you get around the city and beyond. Here is some practical information on transportation in Dublin:

1. Bus: Dublin Bus is the main provider of public transport in Dublin, with an extensive network of routes throughout the city and surrounding areas. The buses run from early morning until late at night, with night buses operating on certain routes. Fares can be paid with cash or with a

Leap Card, a rechargeable smart card that offers discounted fares.

2. Luas: The Luas is Dublin's light rail system, with two lines serving different parts of the city. The Green Line runs from the city center to the suburbs in the south, while the Red Line runs from the city center to the suburbs in the west. The Luas is a quick and convenient way to get around the city, with frequent services running from early morning until late at night. Fares can be paid with cash or with a Leap Card.

3. DART: The DART is Dublin's commuter rail service, running along the coastline from Malahide in the

north to Greystones in the south. The DART offers stunning views of the Irish Sea and the coastline, and is a great way to explore the seaside towns and villages outside of Dublin. Fares can be paid with cash or with a Leap Card.

4. Taxi: Taxis are widely available in Dublin, with ranks located throughout the city center and at major transport hubs such as the airport and train stations. Taxis in Dublin are metered, with fares based on distance and time of day. It is also possible to book a taxi in advance using a smartphone app such as MyTaxi or Hailo.

5. Car rental: If you prefer to explore Dublin and its surrounding areas by car, there are plenty of car rental companies located throughout the city and at the airport. However, driving in Dublin can be challenging, especially during peak traffic hours, and parking can be difficult to find and expensive.

6. Cycling: Dublin has a growing network of cycle lanes and paths, making it a popular choice for cyclists. There are also a number of bike rental companies located throughout the city, with options for both short-term and long-term rentals.

Overall, there are plenty of transportation options in Dublin to suit all budgets and preferences, making it easy to explore the city and beyond.

Money and Tipping

When visiting Dublin, it's important to have an understanding of the local currency and tipping customs. Here is some practical information on money and tipping in Dublin:

1. Currency: The currency used in Dublin is the Euro (€). Banknotes come in denominations of €5, €10, €20, €50, €100, €200, and €500, while coins come in denominations of 1c, 2c, 5c, 10c, 20c, 50c, €1, and €2. ATMs are widely available throughout the city, and credit and debit cards are widely accepted.

2. Tipping: Tipping in Dublin is generally expected in restaurants, cafes, and bars, although it is not mandatory. The standard tip is 10-15% of the total bill, depending on the level of service received. Some restaurants may include a service charge on the bill, in which case additional tipping is not necessary. Tipping for other services, such as hairdressers, taxis, and hotel staff, is also common, but again not mandatory. In general, rounding up to the nearest Euro or leaving small change is a common practice.

3. Exchange rates: If you need to exchange currency, it's best to do so at a bank or currency exchange bureau,

rather than at a hotel or tourist attraction, where the exchange rates may be less favorable. It's also a good idea to check the current exchange rates before traveling, as these can fluctuate daily.

4. Budgeting: Dublin can be an expensive city, especially in the tourist areas. However, there are plenty of budget-friendly options available, such as street food markets, cafes, and hostels. It's a good idea to plan ahead and budget accordingly, taking into account the cost of accommodation, food, transportation, and activities.

5. Credit cards: Credit and debit cards are widely accepted in Dublin,

although it's always a good idea to carry some cash for smaller purchases and to use in places where cards may not be accepted. It's also a good idea to notify your bank or credit card company before traveling, to avoid any issues with card usage.

Overall, having a basic understanding of the local currency and tipping customs can help you to have a smooth and enjoyable trip to Dublin.

Safety and Security

Dublin is generally a safe city for tourists, but it's still important to take certain precautions to ensure your safety and security while visiting. Here is some practical information on safety and security in Dublin:

1. Crime: Like any major city, Dublin has its share of crime, including pickpocketing, theft, and occasional incidents of violent crime. To minimize the risk of becoming a victim of crime, it's important to be aware of your surroundings, especially in busy areas such as the city center, and to keep valuables such as phones and wallets secure.

2. Scams: Tourists in Dublin may be targeted by scams such as fake charity collectors or street performers demanding payment. It's important to be cautious and not to give money to anyone you don't know, and to be aware that some scams may involve distraction techniques to steal valuables.

3. Terrorism: While the threat of terrorism in Dublin is low, it's still important to be vigilant and report any suspicious activity to the authorities. There are also occasional public demonstrations and protests in the city, which can sometimes turn violent.

4. Public transport: Dublin's public transport system is generally safe, but it's important to be aware of your surroundings and to keep your belongings with you at all times. Some areas of the city, particularly at night, may be less safe than others, so it's important to plan your route in advance and to avoid walking alone in unfamiliar areas.

5. Emergency services: In the event of an emergency, dial 112 or 999 to reach the police, fire department, or ambulance service. It's important to have a basic understanding of the local emergency services and to know how

to contact them in case of an emergency.

6. Accommodation: When choosing accommodation in Dublin, it's important to choose a reputable hotel or hostel, and to take basic safety precautions such as locking your door and keeping valuables in a safe.

Overall, Dublin is a relatively safe city for tourists, but it's still important to be aware of your surroundings and to take basic safety precautions to ensure a safe and enjoyable trip.

Conclusion

Final Thoughts and Recommendations

Dublin is a vibrant and historic city that offers visitors a unique blend of culture, history, and modern amenities. As your trip to Dublin comes to a close, here are some final thoughts and recommendations to keep in mind.

Firstly, Dublin is a city that is best explored on foot. While public transportation is available, the city is compact and easy to navigate on foot. Take some time to wander through the city's streets and alleys, explore its historic sites, and soak in the vibrant atmosphere of its neighborhoods.

Secondly, be sure to indulge in Dublin's food and drink scene. From traditional Irish pub fare to innovative cuisine, Dublin has something to offer every palate. Be sure to try some of the city's famous pub grub, such as fish and chips or a hearty Irish stew, and sample some of its local beers and whiskeys.

Thirdly, if you're interested in Irish history and culture, be sure to visit some of the city's museums and galleries. The National Museum of Ireland is a great place to start, with its collection of artifacts and exhibits that showcase the country's rich history. The National Gallery of Ireland is also worth a visit, with its collection of paintings, sculptures, and other artworks.

Finally, if you're looking for some outdoor activities, consider taking a walk through Phoenix Park, the largest urban park in Europe. The park is home to several historic sites, including the Dublin Zoo, the President's residence, and the Victorian People's Flower Gardens.

In conclusion, Dublin is a city that has something to offer everyone, from history buffs to foodies to outdoor enthusiasts. As you prepare to leave this vibrant city, take some time to reflect on your experiences and plan your next trip back. Dublin is a city that will always have more to offer, and you're sure to leave with memories that will last a lifetime.

Dublin Travel Checklist

If you're planning a trip to Dublin, it's important to have a travel checklist to ensure you have everything you need for a comfortable and enjoyable trip. Here are some essential items to include on your Dublin travel checklist:

1. Passport and visa: Make sure you have a valid passport and any necessary visas for your trip.

2. Travel documents: Print out your flight and hotel reservations, as well as any tour or activity bookings you've made in advance.

3. Currency: Bring euros, the currency used in Ireland, or make arrangements to withdraw cash from an ATM once you arrive.

4. Clothing: Dublin's weather can be unpredictable, so pack layers and a raincoat or umbrella. Comfortable walking shoes are also a must for exploring the city on foot.

5. Adapters: Ireland uses the Type G electrical plug, so make sure to bring an adapter if your electronic devices use a different plug type.

6. Mobile phone: Check with your mobile carrier to ensure your phone will work in Ireland. You may also want

to consider purchasing an international data plan.

7. Travel insurance: Consider purchasing travel insurance to protect yourself against unexpected cancellations, medical emergencies, and lost or stolen luggage.

8. Medications: Bring any necessary medications with you, as well as a copy of your prescription and a note from your doctor if necessary.

9. Guidebook or map: Bring a guidebook or map of Dublin to help you navigate the city and plan your itinerary.

10. Camera: Don't forget to bring a camera to capture your memories of Dublin's beautiful architecture, scenery, and attractions.

By including these items on your Dublin travel checklist, you'll be well-prepared for a smooth and enjoyable trip to this vibrant city.